AWESOME SUPER SIMPLE
HABITAT PROJECTS

SUPER SIMPLE

RAIN FOREST

PROJECTS

FUN & EASY ANIMAL ENVIRONMENT ACTIVITIES

CAROLYN BERNHARDT

CONSULTING EDITOR, DIANE CRAIG, M.A./READING SPECIALIST

Super Sandcastle

An Imprint of Abdo Publishing
abdopublishing.com

abdopublishing.com

Published by Abdo Publishing, a division of ABDO, PO Box 398166, Minneapolis, Minnesota 55439. Copyright © 2017 by Abdo Consulting Group, Inc. International copyrights reserved in all countries. No part of this book may be reproduced in any form without written permission from the publisher. Super SandCastle™ is a trademark and logo of Abdo Publishing.

Printed in the United States of America, North Mankato, Minnesota
102016
012017

Editor: Liz Salzmann
Content Developer: Nancy Tuminelly
Cover and Interior Design and Production: Mighty Media, Inc.
Photo Credits: Mighty Media, Inc.; Shutterstock

The following manufacturers/names appearing in this book are trademarks:
Craft Smart®, Crayola®, Elmer's® Glue-All®, Market Pantry™, Sharpie®

Publisher's Cataloging-in-Publication Data

Names: Bernhardt, Carolyn, author.
Title: Super simple rain forest projects: fun & easy animal environment activities / by Carolyn Bernhardt.
Other titles: Fun & easy animal environment activities | Fun and easy animal environment activities
Description: Minneapolis, MN : Abdo Publishing, 2017. | Series: Awesome super simple habitat projects
Identifiers: LCCN 2016944699 | ISBN 9781680784435 (lib. bdg.) | ISBN 9781680797961 (ebook)
Subjects: LCSH: Habitats--Juvenile literature. | Habitat (Ecology)-- Juvenile literature. | Rain forest ecology--Juvenile literature.
Classification: DDC 577.34--dc23
LC record available at http://lccn.loc.gov/2016944699

Super SandCastle™ books are created by a team of professional educators, reading specialists, and content developers around five essential components—phonemic awareness, phonics, vocabulary, text comprehension, and fluency—to assist young readers as they develop reading skills and strategies and increase their general knowledge. All books are written, reviewed, and leveled for guided reading, early reading intervention, and Accelerated Reader™ programs for use in shared, guided, and independent reading and writing activities to support a balanced approach to literacy instruction.

To Adult Helpers

The projects in this book are fun and simple. There are just a few things to remember to keep kids safe. Some projects require the use of nuts or sharp objects. Also, kids may be using messy materials such as glue or paint. Make sure they protect their clothes and work surfaces. Review the projects before starting, and be ready to assist when necessary.

KEY SYMBOLS

Watch for these warning symbols in this book. Here is what they mean.

NUTS!
Some people can get sick if they touch or eat nuts.

SHARP!
You will be working with a sharp object. Get help!

CONTENTS

WILD
RAIN FORESTS!

More than half of the plant and animal **species** on Earth live in rain forests. But rain forests only make up six percent of Earth's surface. That's a lot of life in a small space!

A rain forest has four main layers. The top layer is the emergent layer. This is the tops of the tallest trees. They stick up above the other trees. Emergent layer trees can be 200 feet (60 m) tall! The next layer is the canopy. The trees here are 60 to 150 feet (18 to 46 m) tall. The canopy forms a roof over the rain forest.

EMERGENT LAYER

CANOPY

The layer under the canopy is the understory. It includes the leaves and branches of shorter trees and plants. The bottom layer of a rain forest is the forest floor.

EMERGENT LAYER

CANOPY

UNDERSTORY

FOREST FLOOR

SMALL BUT
MIGHTY!

Rain forests supply us with wood, fruit, coffee, and many other important goods. One-fourth of the world's medicines come from rain forest plants. Rain forests provide us with a lot of things we need. But they are also important animal **habitats**.

There are two main types of rain forest. These are **tropical** rain forests and **temperate** rain forests. Both types get a lot of rain. Tropical rain forests are located close to the equator. This makes them hotter and a little wetter than temperate rain forests.

ORCHIDS IN A
TROPICAL RAIN
FOREST

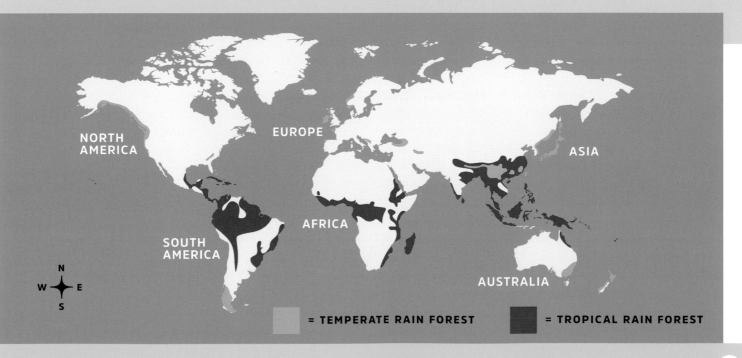

NORTH
AMERICA

EUROPE

ASIA

AFRICA

SOUTH
AMERICA

AUSTRALIA

N
W   E
S

= TEMPERATE RAIN FOREST   = TROPICAL RAIN FOREST

HABITAT
FOOD CHAIN

Every natural **habitat** has a food chain. The food chain shows what each animal eats. When humans harm a habitat, they ruin the food chain's balance. This causes some animals to go hungry.

RAIN FOREST FOOD CHAIN

A food chain has several levels. The animals in one level mostly eat the animals in the level below. But some animals can be on more than one level.

The bottom, or level 1, of a food chain is plants. They make their own food from sunlight, air, and water. Level 2 of a food chain is **herbivores**. Level 3 is **carnivores** that eat herbivores. Level 4 is the top of a food chain. This level is carnivores that eat other carnivores. These animals have few predators.

4

3

2

1

LEVEL 1

RAIN FOREST PLANTS

bamboo trees, banana plants, ferns, fir trees, fungi, moss, orchids

CHIMP CHAMPION

Dr. Jane Goodall began studying chimpanzees in 1960. Very little was known about these animals and their **habitat** then. Goodall discovered much about chimpanzees and their surroundings. She has also been a part of many animal rights groups. Goodall works hard to keep the world's animals safe!

LEVEL 2

RAIN FOREST HERBIVORES

butterflies, deer, fruit bats, grasshoppers, hummingbirds, iguanas, monkeys, parrots, sloths, squirrels

LEVEL 3

RAIN FOREST CARNIVORES

frogs, ocelots, pythons, raccoons, ravens, vampire bats, woodpeckers

LEVEL 4

RAIN FOREST CARNIVORES

anacondas, bears, boa constrictors, cougars, eagles, jaguars, leopards, lynx, owls, wolves

MATERIALS

Here are some of the materials that you will need for the projects in this book.

AIR-DRY CLAY

CARD STOCK

CARDBOARD

CHIA SEEDS

CLEAR GALLON
PLASTIC JUG

CLEAR PACKING
TAPE

CONSTRUCTION
PAPER

CRAFT KNIFE

DINNER KNIFE

FELT

GLUE

HOOK-AND-LOOP
TAPE

MAGAZINES

MARKERS

MOSS

NEWSPAPER

PAINT

PAINT PENS

PAINTBRUSH

PEANUT BUTTER

PENCIL

PRETZEL RODS

SCISSORS

SHOE BOX

SOIL

SPRAY BOTTLE

STRING

TISSUE PAPER

TWIGS

WHITE RECYCLABLE CUP

TINY TREE
TERRARIUM

MATERIALS: clear gallon plastic jug, craft knife, soil, tropical terrarium plants, spray bottle, water, clear packing tape

Rain forests are recyclers! They reuse water over and over again. Rain forest trees and plants store water. Some of this water **evaporates**. It turns into tiny drops in the air. The drops combine with each other in clouds. They become too heavy to stay in the clouds. The water rains down on the rain forest plants. Then the **cycle** starts again!

GROW A SELF-WATERING GARDEN!

① Carefully cut the top third of the bottle off with the craft knife.

② Put some soil in the jug.

③ Place the plants in the soil. Add more soil to cover their roots.

④ Mist the plants with the spray bottle.

⑤ Tape the top of the bottle back on. Remove the cap.

⑥ Place the **terrarium** in a sunny window. Watch rain forest water recycling in action!

FELT BOARD FOREST
OBSERVATORY

MATERIALS: computer, printer, scissors, glue, card stock, hook-and-loop tape, felt (various colors), large sheet of cardboard, word-processing program

Trees in the rain forest live a long time. Some of them can live up to 2,000 years! These trees have a lot of time to grow very tall. Animals live in all layers of the rain forest, from the treetops to the forest floor.

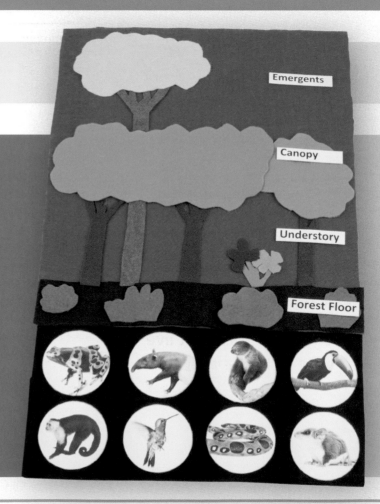

Emergents

Canopy

Understory

Forest Floor

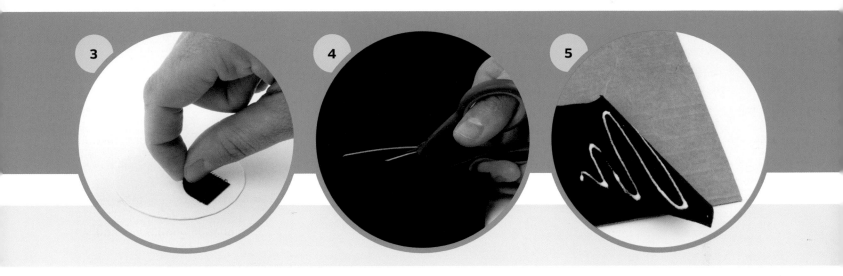

WHAT LIVES WHERE?

① With adult help, **research** the layers of the rain forest. Find facts about the plants and animals that live in each one. Print pictures of the animals that live in the different layers.

② Cut out the animal pictures. Glue each animal to a small piece of card stock.

③ Cut small pieces of scratchy hook-and-loop tape. Stick one to the back of each animal.

④ Cut a rectangle of black felt. It should cover about one-fourth of the cardboard.

⑤ Glue the black felt to one end of the cardboard.

Continued on the next page.

FOREST OBSERVATORY (CONTINUED)

6 Cut a large piece of blue felt. It should cover the rest of the cardboard.

7 Glue the blue felt to the cardboard.

8 Cut a strip of brown felt for the forest floor. Glue it over the bottom edge of the blue felt.

9 Cut some small plants out of felt. Glue them to the forest floor.

10 Cut more rain forest plants out of felt. This includes trees, flowers, and bigger plants. Glue them under the canopy.

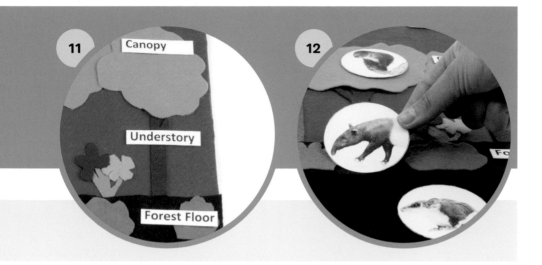

11 Type the names of the layers in a word-processing program. Print out the list. Cut the names apart to make labels. Glue the labels to the board.

12 Place the animals in the levels of the rain forest where they live! Keep extra animals in the black area.

DIGGING DEEPER

Temperate and **tropical** rain forests both have similar layers. But the plants and animals in each rain forest can be different. **Research** the differences between temperate and tropical rain forests. What plants and animals live in each type?

ORCHIDS GROW IN TROPICAL RAIN FORESTS

FIR TREES GROW IN TEMPERATE RAIN FORESTS

ANIMALS
IN THE DARK

MATERIALS: computer, printer, scissors, newspaper, shoe box, paint (three shades of blue), paintbrush, twigs, air-dry clay, tissue paper, glue, pencil, construction paper, moss

Many types of animals and plants live under the canopy layer of the rain forest! The bottom two layers are very dark. This is because the layers above block most of the sun's rays. The canopy also blocks the wind and traps moisture underneath it. This makes the air under the canopy very **humid**.

MAKE A RAIN FOREST SHADOW BOX!

1. With adult help, **research** rain forest animals. Find pictures of those that live in the lower layers.

2. Print out images of the animals. Cut them out. Leave a tab at the bottom if the animal lives on the forest floor.

3. Cover your work surface with newspaper. Set the box on its side. Paint the inside of the box blue. Use the darkest blue on one third of the box. Use a lighter blue on the middle third. Use the lightest blue on the final third. Let it dry.

4. Press a twig into a ball of air-dry clay. This gives it a base. Repeat to make more trees. Let the clay dry.

Continued on the next page.

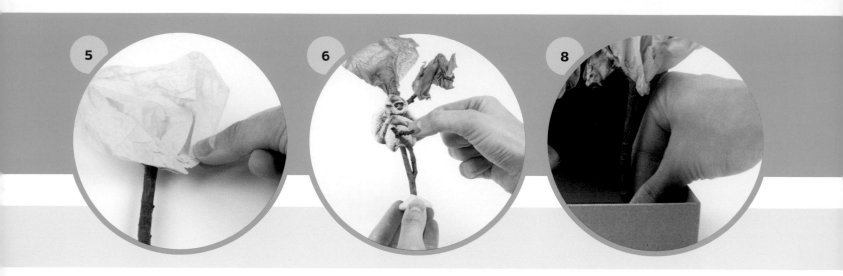

ANIMALS IN THE DARK (CONTINUED)

⑤ Form pieces of tissue paper into treetop shapes. Glue them onto the twigs. Let them dry.

⑥ Glue the animals that live in the understory to lower branches of trees. Let them dry.

⑦ Set the box in the lid with the dark side at the bottom. Tape it in place. Use the pencil to poke 10 to 15 holes in the top of the box. This will let a little light shine into the box.

⑧ Press the tree bases to the bottom of the box and lid.

9   Cut grass shapes out of construction paper.

10   Glue grass to the bottom of the box and lid around the trees.

11   Fold the tabs on the ground animals back. Glue them to the bottom of the box and lid.

12   Cover any empty space on the bottom with moss.

13   Place your shadow box in a sunny window. Observe how the light shines through the holes in the top of the box. How much light reaches the understory and the forest floor? How do the trees affect this?

DIGGING DEEPER

The canopy of the rain forest is thick with leaves! It blocks almost all of the sunlight. However, a few little rays of sunlight peek through the leaves. This small amount of sunlight is just enough to let the right plants and animals grow. It keeps the rain forest alive!

COLORFUL ANIMALS

MATERIALS: computer, printer, glue, card stock, magazines, scissors

Rain forests are found on almost every continent! The plants and animals in these forests vary greatly. Many rain forest plants and animals are brightly colored. There are different reasons for these colors.

MAKE AN ANIMAL MOSAIC!

① With adult help, **research** rain forest animals. Choose one that has bright colors.

② Find and print a picture of your chosen animal. Glue the picture to a sheet of card stock.

③ Cut small, colored pieces out of magazines. Look for colors that match the colors of your animal.

④ Glue the pieces to the pictures to create a **mosaic**!

DIGGING DEEPER

A flower's color can **attract** bees, butterflies, and other insects. These insects **pollinate** the flower. For a reptile such as a snake or lizard, its colors are **camouflage**. For a frog or insect, the colors are a warning that it tastes bad or is toxic. This keeps predators from wanting to eat it. And a bird's colors help it attract a mate.

COLLAPSIBLE
FOOD CHAIN

MATERIALS: computer,
4 white recyclable cups,
markers, paint pens,
pencil, string, scissors

The Amazon Rain Forest is huge!
It is bigger than most countries.
There are many animals in the
Amazon Rain Forest food chain.
Each animal in this food chain plays
an important role in keeping the
ecosystem in balance. See pages
8 and 9 for more about rain forest
food chains.

MAKE A FOOD CHAIN OUT OF CUPS!

① **With adult help, research** the Amazon Rain Forest food chain. Make lists of the animals and plants in each level. Include what each animal eats.

② Turn the cups upside down. Trace or draw an animal or plant on each cup. Choose something from each level of the food chain.

③ Color the drawings with markers and paint pens.

④ Write the animal or plant's name on the rim of the cup.

⑤ Write facts about each animal or plant on the back of its cup. Include the things it eats or what it needs to grow.

Continued on the next page.

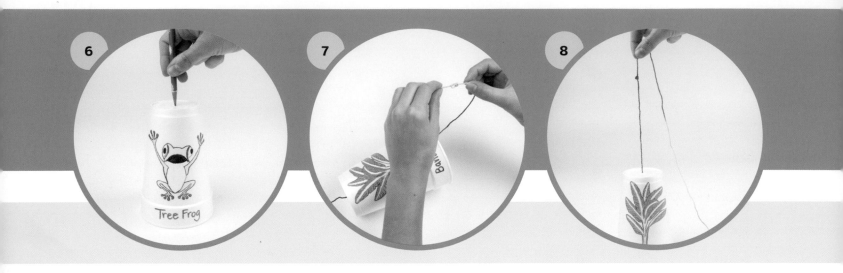

COLLAPSIBLE FOOD CHAIN (CONTINUED)

6 Poke a hole in the bottom of each cup.

7 Thread the string through the hole in the cup for the bottom of the food chain. Tie a large knot in the string inside the cup.

8 Tie another knot in the string a few inches above the bottom of the cup.

9 Thread the string up through the cup for the next level of the food chain.

10 Repeat steps 8 and 9 to add the last two cups. Make sure the level 4 animal is on top.

11 Cut the string a few inches above the top cup.

DIGGING DEEPER

Food chains are a way for energy to spread to all wildlife in a rain forest. This energy starts with the sun. Plants use the sun's energy to grow. They pass some of the sun's energy to the animals that eat them. Then those animals pass some of the energy to their predators. That is how the sun's energy spreads throughout the rain forest food chain!

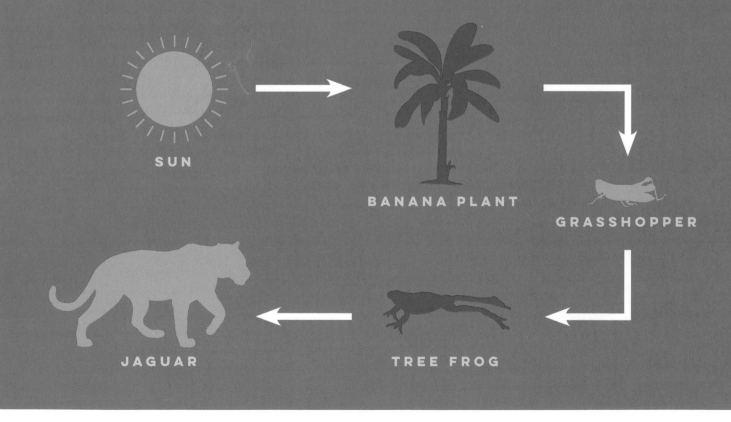

SUN

BANANA PLANT

GRASSHOPPER

JAGUAR

TREE FROG

CHIMP TOOLS

MATERIALS: chia seeds, bowl, dinner knife, peanut butter, pretzel rods

Did you know that humans are not the only living things to use tools? Chimpanzees make and use tools too! One way they use tools is to get ants out of their nests. A chimp will poke a stick into a nest. The ants cling to the stick. Then the chimp pulls the stick out and eats the ants.

SNACK LIKE A CHIMP!

1. Put some chia seeds in a bowl. These are the ants.

2. Spread peanut butter over one end of a pretzel rod.

3. Dip the peanut butter end into the chia seeds.

4. Repeat steps 2 and 3 to make more ant-covered tools. Enjoy your snack!

DIGGING DEEPER

Scientists used to think that only humans made and used tools. But Dr. Jane Goodall discovered that chimpanzees use tools too! Chimps drink water, eat food, and clean themselves with tools. Chimpanzees make their tools out of sticks, leaves, and rocks. They learn how to make tools by watching one another.

CONCLUSION

Rain forests are full of interesting plants and animals. They also provide us with foods and medicines. Unfortunately, human activity and pollution are slowly destroying the rain forests. This book is the first step in learning more about rain forests and how to protect them. There is so much more to find out!

Do you live near a rain forest? Have you ever visited one? Go to the library to **research** the world's rain forests.

Or have an adult help you research rain forests **online**. Learn about what you can do to help preserve rain forests!

QUIZ

1. How many layers does a rain forest have?

2. There are two main types of rain forest.
   TRUE OR FALSE?

3. Who discovered that chimpanzees use tools?

THINK ABOUT IT!

What do you think is the most important rain forest plant or animal? Why is it important?

Answers: 1. Four   2. True   3. Dr. Jane Goodall

GLOSSARY

attract – to cause someone or something to come near.

camouflage – a method of hiding from sight by using a disguise or protective coloring to blend in to the surroundings.

carnivore – an animal that eats mainly meat.

cycle – a series of events that happen over and over again.

ecosystem – a group of plants and animals that live together in nature and depend on each other to survive.

evaporate – to change from a liquid into a gas.

habitat – the area or environment where a person or animal usually lives.

herbivore – an animal that eats mainly plants.

humid – damp or moist, especially relating to air.

mosaic – a decorative design made up of many small parts.

online – connected to the Internet.

pollinate – to carry pollen from one flower to another.

research – to find out more about something.

species – a group of related living beings.

temperate – located where the weather is never very hot or very cold.

terrarium – a clear enclosure for keeping and observing small animals and plants.

tropical – located in the hot, wet areas of Earth.